AMERICAN SILVER

1. Porringer made by John Coney, Boston, showing an unusual treatment of handle.

AMERICAN SILVER

BY

MILLICENT STOW

GRAMERCY PUBLISHING COMPANY
NEW YORK

IN APPRECIATION

No book, however small, can be written without the assistance of many generous people. This help has come to me from the written word, from museums, large and small, from collectors, and from those thousands of people who have written to me for information about their old silver. These letters to my column of questions and answers in the New York *Sun* (now the *World-Telegram and Sun*) have revealed what the average person wants to know about silver, and so have been a guide to me in this discussion. I am grateful too to those dealers in old silver who have made a profession of their work and have been kind about sharing their knowledge with me.

It would be impossible to list all those who have helped me in the past with their knowledge, who have shared their collections, lent their photographs, but I am especially grateful to Mr. and Mrs. Stanley B. Ineson; Dr. George B. Cutten; Dr. John Marshall Phillips; Henry F. du Pont; Alice Winchester; Helen Burr Smith; Mrs. John Russel Hastings; C. Louise Avery; Stephen G. C. Ensko; Edwin J. Hipkiss; V. Isabelle Miller; R. W. G. Vail; Kathryn C. Buhler, and especially my husband, Charles Messer Stow, for his patience and fortitude during this endeavor.

New York City   MILLICENT STOW

6.

CONTENTS

I. SILVER OF THE COLONIES

The history of American silver parallels in a most interesting way the social development of the country. The first silver used by the Colonists was simple and useful, but as the country grew and prospered, the demand for more and finer pieces increased. By the time of the Revolution, wealthy Colonists were living as graciously as their contemporaries in England, and after we became a nation, the work of American silver-smiths reached great heights, which continued into the first quarter of the nineteenth century. Then the machine won the battle of decoration over design, and ugliness tried to hide behind prettiness.

In the early seventeenth century, when the first settlers came to Virginia and New England, they had little room in their small ships for luxuries. No doubt a few of the more prosperous brought along some of their treasures and these must have included silver. Precious metals have always been a form of exchange, and good to have for emergencies. The earliest silver brought to this country was English and Dutch. This may have been melted down in later years by Colonial silver-

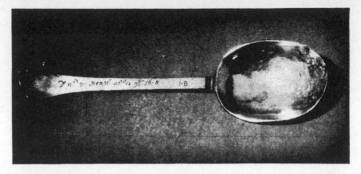

2. *Memorial spoon made by Cornelius Vander Burgh, N. Y., dated 1678.*

3. *Standing cup by Hull and Sanderson. Donated "to ye. Ch. of Rehoboth, 1674." Garvan Collection, Yale University.*

smiths and made into pieces we now recognize as American.

The early years in the new country were hard. There were houses to build and lands to till. For some time life was a battle for existence. There was little need for luxuries and little means with which to procure them.

History records how the country prospered. Shipping was established with England, the West Indies, Spain, and Portugal and trade brought silver coins from these foreign lands. A class of wealthy shipping merchants developed. The first luxuries were imported from England, but soon local craftsmen were needed and cabinetmakers and silversmiths opened shops in the cities where they copied the designs of English craftsmen.

The early silversmiths were naturally English. It took seven years of apprenticeship to develop a silversmith in this country. A lad born in the Colonies would be apprenticed at fourteen to a master who had recently come from London. The boy stayed with his master until he was twenty-one and then he too became a master silversmith, if he had proved his skill.

Because the settlers of New England were religious, the first silver made there was usually for churches and reflected the simple tastes of the people. On the whole English designs were followed, but gradually certain characteristics developed which made New England silver different from that made in New York, Philadelphia, and other parts of the country. Even today many

4. *Cup by John Dixwell, Boston (1680–1725).*
Given to the Church of Christ in Norwich in
1722. Museum of Fine Arts, Boston.

5. *Two-handled bowl by Cornelius Vander*
Burgh, N. Y. (1652–1699). Over nine inches
across, without the handles.

12.

6. Inside of Vander Burgh bowl showing exquisite detail of workmanship.

New England churches are proud owners of early silver that has been treasured for generations. Occasionally a town or region holds an exhibition and it is always a surprise to see what fine pieces are still owned by even the smaller country parishes.

Although New York and Philadelphia designs usually followed those of the London silversmiths of the period, early New York silver shows the influence of the Dutch ancestry of its makers. There is more applied decoration and greater boldness in design. The list of New York smiths includes such Dutch names as Gerrit Onkelbag, Peter Van Dyke, Henricus Boelen, and Jacobus Vanderspiegel; in Boston appeared names like John Coney, Jacob Hurd, Robert Sanderson, Jeremiah Dummer, and John Burt. These men

13.

7. *Bowl by Jacob Hurd, Boston (1702–1758). Name of owner and date. Probably a christening bowl.*

with English names thought as the English did. However even in the early days of the Colonies an interesting mixture of nationalities was indicated, particularly in the names of Huguenot silversmiths—Le Roux, Boudinot, Goelet, Du Bois,

8. *Well-designed cup by Isaac Anthony, Newport, R. I. (1690–1773). Type made about 1715 for home or church use.*

9. *Caudle cup by John Coney, Boston (1655– 1722).*

and Soumaine. Each smith added something from his own country to his work, thus developing in America a wonderful tradition of fine design and workmanship.

In the beginning the Colonists used what utensils they could make and the few they had brought with them. Probably the first plates and perhaps even the first spoons were of wood. This early ware was known as treen, a term derived from the word trees; treen was the simplest form of the most plentiful material. But there were also pewterers among the early settlers and they were soon making spoons and plates of pewter.

Until 1652 the Colonies had no currency. In that year, John Hull, a silversmith from London, was made mintmaster by the General Court of Massachusetts. He was probably the first silversmith to work in Boston. Hull with his partner, Robert Sanderson, produced the willow-tree, oaktree, and pine-tree shilling used in the New England Colonies until 1683. This partnership also produced many fine pieces of silver with Hull and Sanderson marks. In the Mabel Brady Garvan collection at Yale University is one of their spoons, the earliest known American one, and also a small dram cup.

The coins made by Hull and Sanderson were intended only for New England. But silver had a way of getting around even in those days for it was a medium of exchange. It was also worth stealing and a merchant with money at home or in his place of business had cause for worry.

It is at this point that the silversmith becomes an important member of the community. To him the prosperous man took his coins and had them melted down and fashioned into household articles—spoons, tankards, and porringers. After melting the coins, the silversmith refined the metal, and poured it into a skillet to form a flat block of silver. The block was hammered out to the desired thickness and worked into whatever article the patron ordered. The metal was worked while cold, but was repeatedly heated over charcoal to prevent brittleness and to make it tougher. This process was called annealing.

A finished article was polished by rubbing with pumice and then with a burnisher. This method did not cut away the surface but simply rubbed it smooth while leaving some hammer marks. Collectors feel that these marks add to the charm of a piece of old silver. The surface of antique silver has a patina rather like that of fine

10. Two-handled bowl with decorated panels, by Cornelius Kierstede, N. Y. (1674–1757).

old wood and this increases with years of hand-rubbing. Furthermore, since each piece was made wholly by hand, no two are ever quite alike.

A merchant, who had his coins made into household articles, had them engraved with initials or crest. In this way his wealth in silver was useful; it was still an investment, but it was not likely to be stolen, for initialed silver was fairly easy to trace. However, old records show that sometimes articles of silver were stolen, but after advertisements appeared with a detailed description of some family piece, it was usually returned and the thief punished.

While the North was developing skillful craftsmen who made things in the English manner, the South imported nearly everything, ordering luxuries and even necessities from London agents. These were paid for in tobacco, and when crops were good, more luxuries were imported. As a result of this policy there were few important sil-

11. LEFT: *Porringer made by Samuel Vernon, Newport, R. I. (1683–1737).* RIGHT: *Porringer made by Jeremiah Dummer, Boston (1645–1718), with the simple handles of the early period.*

versmiths in the South until well into the eighteenth century. Even in Williamsburg, capital of the Virginia Colony during the early eighteenth century, there was not a silversmith of importance and all fine articles were imported from London.

The first articles made by American silversmiths were spoons. Knives and forks were not in general use until the eighteenth century. Today American spoons of the seventeenth century are rare. Yet many must have been made. However, they got such hard use they doubtless had to be melted down and were then made into spoons of later design or possibly into other articles. Whatever the reason for scarcity, the few early spoons known today are in museums or private collections.

12. Very rare dram cup. Hull and Sanderson, Boston, between 1652 and 1675. Handle shows continental influence. Garvan Collection.

One fine early spoon with the mark of Hull and Sanderson is in the Essex Institute in Salem, Massachusetts. It has a large bowl rather like a fig, and the handle is a straight piece. This type, usually called the Puritan spoon, is the earliest form known in this country.

After the spoon, the porringer, small bowl, and tankard were made for food and drink. Liquor in some form was generally enjoyed, even by the clergy. Those who could afford it had these articles made of silver; others used pewter, or even pottery. The tankards were usually made large to hold the quantities of liquor apparently necessary in a cold climate. Tankards, porringers, and bowls were also used in the churches and

13. Tankard made by Robert Sanderson, Boston (1638–1693).

have been found in the collections of early church silver.

PORRINGERS

Very likely you know someone who has inherited a porringer, or perhaps you own one yourself. They were such personal pieces of silver that they were usually handed down from one

14. Tankard made by Edward Winslow, Boston (1669–1753). Fine example of early Boston type.

generation to another instead of being sold. Large and small porringers were used during the seventeenth and eighteenth centuries in almost every home. The people who could not afford silver had them made of pewter. The English porringers had two handles and were supposed to have been used for bleeding bowls by barber surgeons.

15. Tankard by Adrian Bancker, N. Y. (1702–1772). Cut-card decoration at bottom and fine engraving.

Probably porringers were made first in this country by the New England silversmiths. These early specimens had only one handle. No one knows just what they originally were made to contain, but history tells us that porringers were used for almost every kind of food from bread and milk to vegetables. Before sugar bowls were

16. Dome-top tankard by John Noyes, Boston (1674–1749). Good example of simple designs used by Boston silversmiths.

made porringers were also used to hold sugar.

Perhaps you have noticed two sets of initials on some of the silver porringers. This is quite common and is generally the mark of a bride and groom, because nearly every young couple had at least one porringer for the new home. Porringers were also given for christening gifts, and many a small child who lived and died before this country became a nation ate his food from one of the porringers you see today in your museum.

*17. Tankard by Jacob Hurd, Boston, about 1735.
"I. Hurd," showing the old form of J, at top
near domed cover.*

Porringers were made in all sizes and depths.
Sometimes the sides flared, sometimes they swelled
out and then turned in again at the top. The
earliest type had simple handles, almost crude in
design. Later handles were more ornate, and the
study of their designs is particularly interesting.
There are rarely two alike.

18. Rare tankard made by Bartholomew Schaats, N. Y. (1670–1758). Fine decorative details.

TANKARDS

Silver tankards were made in this country from the seventeenth to the nineteenth century. The earliest type had a broad flat base, straight tapering sides, and a flat lid with a thumbpiece to raise it. The handle was S-shaped and ended in a shield-shaped end or tip. Lip and base were usually molded. Sometimes this molding had a line of leaves or other embellishment. Often there were molded ornaments on the back of the handle.

19. Can or mug made by John Coney, Boston, with the simplicity and sturdiness favored in New England.

Later styles show one or more bands on the body of the tankard. The cover was rounded out with a finial. The end of the handle was made in the form of a cherub, eagle, or other decorative device.

Tankards vary in size, but the earliest types are usually large. As in all silver, a tendency toward height and slenderness appeared in the late eighteenth century. The tankards also grew higher and more graceful, and the body was beautifully curved.

Study carefully the various thumbpieces on tankards. Although they were for use, the silver-

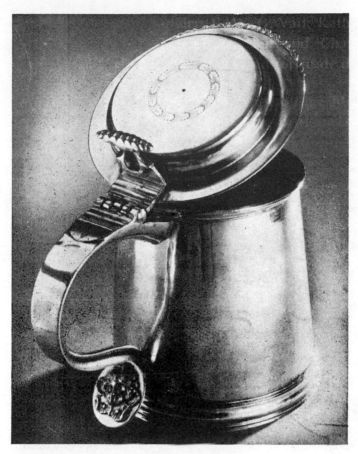

20. *Tankard by Henricus Boelen, N. Y. (1697–1755). A fine example of early New York workmanship.*

smith combined use with beauty when he made them. It is interesting to note where tankards were made and to discover the details used repeatedly by one maker or by makers in one section of the country.

Tankards made in New England are usually simpler than those from New York, where de-

*21. Tankard by William Cowell, Jr., Boston
(1713–1761). An example of simplicity of Boston
designs.*

signs were essentially sturdy. Tankards made by
craftsmen with Dutch background were often
ornamented with a decoration known as cut-card
work—small strips of applied silver suggesting
lace. With a little study it is easy to recognize
these regional characteristics.

22. Tankard by Peter Van Dyke, N. Y. (1684–1751). Coin in cover, a common decoration in Germany, later in Holland.

TEAPOTS AND TEA SETS

By the beginning of the eighteenth century silver articles were in more general use. There was more money to spend and more silversmiths to work, and also new needs for household pieces. About 1650 tea was introduced into England, but

23. Unusual tankard by Samuel Vernon, Newport, R. I. (1683–1735). Dolphin thumbpiece. Unlike Boston and New York tankards.

24. Pear-shaped teapot by Benjamin Burt, son of John Burt, Boston (1729–1805).

25. Teapot by Jacob Hurd, Boston (1702–1758). Only six and one-quarter inches high, beautiful engraving.

it was very expensive and only the wealthy could afford it. In his diary Pepys mentions trying it for the first time in 1660. When tea reached the Colonies few liked it, and it is told that many boiled it as if it were a vegetable and ate the leaves with butter. But in time tea became fashionable in London, where it was served Chinese fashion from china teapots and tiny china cups, and with no silver appointments.

The first English silver teapot, which still exists in the Victoria and Albert Museum, looks like a Chinese porcelain wine pot. It even has a detachable cover and is very small, for tea was still expensive. When one silversmith made a new object, however, others copied it so teapots were soon being made to order and tea-drinking in London became a social custom.

26. Teapot by Peter Van Dyke, N. Y. (1684–1751). A sturdy but graceful design favored by New York makers.

The American Colonists, following the London vogue, also learned to take tea and demanded teapots. Some of the early silver ones show how well Colonial silversmiths kept their clients up-to-date. Like the first English pots, early Colonial counterparts were small, some like a ball, and usually with a lovely crest or cypher engraved to indicate a family name. Coffee and chocolate pots also were made as these beverages became

27. *Footed sauceboat by William Simpkins, Boston (1704–1780). Shows beginning of table elegance in Boston.*

28. *Teapot by Myer Myers, N. Y. (1723–1795). This type of teapot was popular in New York.*

*29. Very lovely teapot by Simeon Soumaine,
N. Y. Born in London in 1685, worked in New
York 1706 to 1750.*

popular, but not until well into the eighteenth
century were there complete sets such as we use
today. There were silver pots, but no one used
sugar or cream for some time, so there was no
need for the sugar bowl and creamer. These were
added late in the century.

Old silver, bearing maker's marks and the
name or crest of a family, has always been a delight to student and collector. Names or initials
give clues to families which can often be traced
in wills and church or court records. With a specific maker's initials and the name of the owner,
it has even been possible to learn much about the
date and origin of a piece, and some articles of
considerable historical significance have been dis-
covered.

30. Creamer made by Cary Dunn, New York, about 1775–1780.

Sugar was advertised in the Boston *News-Letter* in 1724 at three shillings a pound. This was rather expensive for the average household and explains why so little sugar was used with tea. For cooking, molasses and sirup served as sweetening. When sugar was brought in from the West Indies, it was in the form of a cone weighing eight to ten pounds and it was done up in a dark blue paper. (This the thrifty housewife saved to use as a dye for her wool and cotton materials.) To break up the cone a utensil was used that looked rather like a nutcracker with cutting edges.

31. Very rare standing salt by Edward Winslow, Boston. Museum of Fine Arts, Boston.

As sugar became cheaper and more households could afford it, it was used in tea and coffee. Now a container was necessary, which the silversmith supplied along with the tea or coffee pot, although some households used a porringer or a small silver or even china bowl for sugar. Then something was needed to take the sugar from the bowl and silver tongs came into fashion. The first ones were called nippers and worked like scissors.

32. Rare sugar or sweetmeat box by Edward Winslow, Boston, dated 1702. This type made by John Coney and Edward Winslow.

Later tongs were made in one piece. Then as milk and cream came into general use with coffee and tea, a small pitcher, usually called a creamer, was needed for the table and was made by the silversmith and often in a design to match pot and sugar bowl.

SILVER BOXES

Most of the little boxes that you see in collections of silver were designed for gifts rather than for actual use, like certain objects sold today. When you observe the elaborate decoration of many little boxes, remember that they were made at a time when women wore brocades and wigs, and men dressed in silks and satins and wore

33. Rare silver box by Francis Richardson, Philadelphia (1681–1729). Earliest lids separate; later are hinged.

embroidered waistcoats. Among the luxuries of the early days were sweetmeat boxes. These were usually elaborate and costly. A few museums have examples of these beautiful boxes made by Coney and Winslow, two of the seventeenth-century silversmiths. These early pieces were so exquisitely made it is hard to believe that such fine work was done in the early primitive years of our history.

Most of the boxes shown today are products of the eighteenth century and date from after the Revolution. They vary in size and use. Many of them have sentimental lines, with the owner's and sometimes the donor's initials. There are tiny patch boxes for the dots of black court plaster which were a necessary part of milady's toilet, and snuffboxes for the gentlemen of fashion who used snuff. There are also presentation boxes of silver and silver gilt that were given to prominent citizens of the day with appropriate inscriptions. Some of the most skillful silversmiths of all time made little silver boxes for all sorts of uses. Many show engraving equal to that on the finest large pieces of household silver.

It was the custom to give a child a fine christening spoon, and this was usually marked with the name and date of birth. Such spoons are important for the definite records they provide. This is also true of funeral spoons which were given to the pallbearers of a prominent citizen. They usually bore the name of the deceased, the date of death, and the name of the recipient. These spoons are rarities today. Silver was also often given to bride and bridegroom and was usually marked with the initials of both and sometimes with the date of marriage. Such marked silver throws light on our ancestors and is valuable in tracing family trees.

There was need at first for a quite small spoon to use with the tiny china cups. So the silversmiths made a type smaller than the modern teaspoon but a bit larger than what we call a demitasse spoon. These little objects are charming and a collector of American silver is pleased indeed when he adds one or more to his collection. (See Plate 81 ff. for Spoon Designs, 1650–1825.)

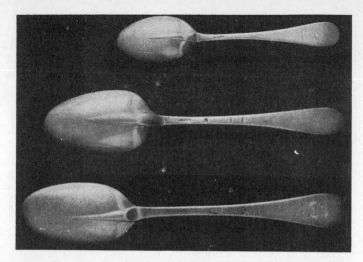

34. American rattail spoons of early 1700s. Prized by collectors. Collection of Mr. and Mrs. Stanley B. Ineson.

35. American rattail spoons with interesting detail on backs. Collection of Mr. and Mrs. Stanley B. Ineson.

36. Rare sucket fork by Bartholomew Le Roux, N. Y. For imported fruits in thick sirup. Collection of Dr. George B. Cutten.

KNIVES AND FORKS

By the middle of the eighteenth century, living in Colonial cities, following that of London, was gracious, indeed, and often luxurious. Colonial governors, familiar with the fashions in England and the Continent, brought new concepts of living to the people. Although few American silversmiths made knives and forks in quantity until the latter part of the eighteenth century, these were imported from England and were usually of steel with bone, ivory, or perhaps silver handles. Sheffield and Birmingham, noted for their fine steel, produced most of the steel household articles brought to the Colonies.

The silver knives and forks we take for granted today were not common even in England until the late seventeenth century. The first known all-silver fork made there bears the date 1632 and is so rare and valuable that it is now in the Vic-

41.

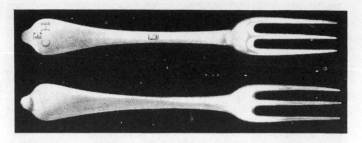

37. *Very rare American fork by Joseph Goldthwaite, Boston (1706–1780).*

toria and Albert Museum in London. It has two tines and a long narrow handle.

In early days only the nobles had knives, which served a double purpose—for eating and for killing either man or beast. They were usually carried in a sheath and were made of the finest steel with handles that ranged from iron to gold, often inlaid and set with precious stones. Every age has its amenities and it was the custom for the noble to wipe his knife off carefully with a fine linen napkin before he put it into the salt dish.

Italy is credited with introducing forks in the sixteenth century, but it was not until early in the seventeenth that an Englishman, Thomas Coryat, saw the nobles there eating with forks. He had one made for himself and took it back to England, but his friends laughed at him and thought him effeminate and history does not record whether or not Coryat continued to use his fork.

Always ahead of his time was Samuel Pepys, the famous columnist of the seventeenth century. We are grateful to him for keeping his diary so

38. Very rare silver plate with engraved rim by John Coney, Boston (1655–1722). Initials suggest wedding silver.

well. In it he records that he bought forks, but Pepys was a rich and fashionable gentleman, and because he had forks, it does not follow that everyone else in London used them at the time. In fact it was quite a while before knives and forks were common there and much longer before they became the fashion here.

THE "GOLDEN AGE" OF THE COLONIES

But prosperity in the Colonies brought with it a desire for better homes and then for better appointments. The people began to live well and in

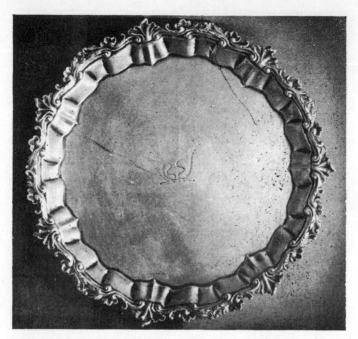

39. Lovely tray with Beekman crest made by Samuel Tingley, New York, who was working in 1754.

40. Footed salver or tray by Nicholas Roosevelt, N. Y. (1715–1771). Very rare, especially with such detail.

*41. Silver caster made by John Coney, Boston
(1655–1722). Museum of Fine Arts, Boston.*

somber New England the wealthy eighteenth-
century folk were chided by the clergy for their
luxurious tastes. Life in New York and Philadelphia was always gayer, and even the Quakers had
fine homes and furnishings.

The simple designs of earlier days were followed in the mid-eighteenth century by more

42. Punch strainer by John Clark, Boston and Salem (1750–1770). Perforations indicate owner —"Jabez Bowen, 1766, Providence."

elaborate forms. This time is often called the Golden Age of the Colonies. Now silver design, like that of furniture, was affected by the work of Thomas Chippendale, the fashionable cabinet-maker of London who made elaborate furniture for the nobility and wealthy people of Britain. He borrowed French, Chinese, and Gothic motifs and even mixed them sometimes. In this age of elegance, silver reflected the wealth of the day and few silversmiths made simple pieces. Everything was heavy with ornament. True, it was beautiful and made by expert craftsmen, but ornament was soon to give way to bad taste.

Meanwhile two important events changed the styles which England and the Colonies followed. Excavation began at Herculaneum and Pompeii, cities buried by Vesuvius in 79 A.D., and the Scottish architect, Robert Adam, went to Italy to study. All Europe took immense interest in these excavations, which uncovered the forgotten classical world. Robert Adam was particularly af-

*43. Beaker by Isaac Hutton, Albany, N. Y.,
1810 to 1815, Greek influence in key design. Albany Institute of History and Art.*

fected. He returned to London to practice
architecture with his head full of classic motifs,
and began to use the style of ancient Greece in his
houses. Robert and his brother, James, probably
had more influence on the design of the day than
any other designer. They employed cabinetmakers, sculptors, painters, even silversmiths to
carry out their ideas.

This new inspiration, this extreme simplicity
of line and the fine proportions of the classic
style appealed to the new nation. Silver was now
fashioned in straight structural lines. It was em-

44. Beaker by Isaac Hutton, contemporary of Paul Revere, Albany, N. Y., about 1790. Albany Institute of History and Art

bellished with delicately engraved ornament, the simple motifs of the urn and swag.

The designs used by American silversmiths at this time were similar to those of England, but the people liked to believe the designs were as new as the nation and the silversmiths helped them think they were right. In 1790 Joseph Anthony, Jr., a Philadelphia smith, advertised silver of "entire new patterns," yet these were much like those in vogue in London.

The spoon at this period was made in all sizes with a pointed bowl and turned-down handle. It was usually plain except for a script monogram or the popular form of ornament known as bright-cut engraving, a delicate shallow pattern of zigzag lines around the edge, or an initialed medallion on the handle. The backs of spoons at this time often had an ornament in relief—a simple drop, an acanthus leaf, or a dove holding an olive branch in its beak. The dove motif was especially appealing to the Quakers.

The early silversmith learned his trade in every detail. He melted silver coins, rolled the resulting mass of silver into a flat piece, and then raised it with his hammers to some beautiful form. If he did not do all the work himself, he had at hand a workman whom he had trained to do at least part of the process for him. But the master craftsman required the finished product to be of such quality that he could be proud to put his stamp upon each piece, either his initials or his name. He stood back of every article that left his shop. Silver-making was highly specialized.

Gradually in various communities little shops sprang up where spoons were produced in quantity. Then these little shops made spoons for jewelers who had *their* names stamped on the product instead of the name of the maker. On this account many spoons are found today with names not listed in any book of American silver marks. The change in marking took place after 1830 when the machine was beginning to be used for all types of work and the day of the expert craftsman was for the most part at an end. The eagle also appeared on the backs of Philadelphia

45. *Mug by Philip Syng, Jr., working in Philadelphia from 1726 to 1789, but born in Ireland in 1703.*

spoons. The American eagle, taken from the United States Seal, was now a popular decoration on other silver as well.

The coffin-end spoon also became the style. This type can never be mistaken for any other design because the handle resembles an old-type wooden coffin. The death of Washington is believed to have made this design a vogue, although universal mourning had long been a mania. Tablespoons, mustard spoons, salt, and dessert spoons, as well as ladles and forks were made in this severe style which was often brightened by a bit of engraving for initials or a monogram.

46. Mug made by the younger Joseph Edwards,
Boston (1737–1783), dated 1765.

The tankard was going out of fashion: it was
no longer good taste to drink to excess and the
temperance movement was having its effect on
the new country—and on silver.

II. SILVER IN THE NEW NATION

After the Revolution the new country was on its own politically and also artistically to a far greater degree than before. During the war there was no trade with England and the Colonists were unaware of new trends across the ocean. Here, there was little opportunity to develop the crafts. As in all periods of stress, only necessities were made and even American silversmiths turned out ammunition. Pewter, brass, and copper were melted down and doubtless many pieces of silver were sacrificed to the Cause.

Many men and women who did not approve the break with Britain fled to Canada, and afterward to England. Often they took their silver with them. Some of these pieces, made by Colonial craftsmen, have been found in recent years in England. A beautiful sugar box made by Edward Winslow turned up in England a few years ago. This type of sugar or sweetmeat box was rare even in the early days and only a few of them have been found. This one had been taken to England during the Revolution. It is now back in this country in a private collection. When peace came, there was again interest in the styles of the mother country, for habit is strong and cabinetmakers and silversmiths again wanted to know what was fashionable in London.

Two new cabinetmakers—Thomas Sheraton and George Hepplewhite—had become fashionable there and were influencing silver as well as other arts and crafts. Both men had published books of designs which found their way to the new nation. By the end of the eighteenth century, silversmiths here were fashioning beautiful pieces in the classic manner with the festoons, urns, and swags introduced by the brothers Adam and included in the Sheraton and Hepplewhite books. Thus began the delicate and dignified period of American design that was to continue into the Machine Age. It is perhaps the type of design that the average person prefers today, if he has not bowed to what is called Contemporary or Modern. It is the style that includes the lovely work of Duncan Phyfe, the celebrated cabinetmaker of New York City. It is also the period of the work of Paul Revere, who skillfully used similar classic designs.

SILVER OF PAUL REVERE

Why is the name of Paul Revere so popular when equally skilled silversmiths are only known to museums and collectors? Perhaps because unlike other craftsmen Paul had a press agent in Longfellow. The poem that immortalized his ride, also made famous his name. His father, Apollos Rivoire, a Huguenot, had come to this

47. Globular teapot by the elder Paul Revere, working in Boston 1725 to 1754. P. Revere is stamped twice on base.

country and been apprenticed to John Coney, a famous silversmith and said to have been the best Boston ever produced. The family name, Rivoire, was changed to the English version, Revere, since Apollos was working for an Englishman.

The son Paul was born in Boston in 1735. Apprenticed to his father, who had learned his craft well with Coney, he was able at nineteen, upon his father's death, to take over the shop. The Reveres were important in Boston and like other silversmiths were active in civic affairs. Paul as a youth joined the local artillery and served against the French at Crown Point in the French and Indian War. After the Revolution, he came back to the silver shop and worked at his craft. He was not only an expert smith but also a skilled engraver and one of the few craftsmen who could complete a piece of silver, even to the engraved

54.

48. Teapot with straight spout and fine engraved decorations, made by the elder Paul Revere.

decoration. Many museums have examples of his work and every visitor interested in old silver wants to see them. Paul Revere worked best in the classic tradition of Adam. His lovely tea and coffee pots usually have graceful engravings of festoons and swags, and the finials are beautifully wrought, sometimes in pineapple form.

In Revere's time many silversmiths were using the china pieces of the day as models. It was the period of the tall Liverpool pitcher which Revere copied so well in his famous water pitchers, some of them plain, some engraved. Chinese Export Ware, often miscalled Chinese Lowestoft, was then in fashion and Revere copied the small, stylized, helmet pitcher in silver.

He made bowls of all sizes, some with inscriptions historically valuable today. It takes a real craftsman to make a perfect bowl and Revere

49. Tankard by Paul Revere, the patriot, Boston (1735–1818).

was able to make decoration an intrinsic element of each piece, for he was a master of subtlety. His best pieces are simple and restrained and perhaps that was the secret of their popularity. Revere lived only until 1818 and so escaped designing when popular demand would have required over ornamentation, which doubtless would have disturbed him greatly.

50. Teapot by Paul Revere, showing fluted oval shape and delicate engraving.

51. Teapot by Paul Revere, the patriot, made in 1785. (Cover illustration).

52. Goblet of simple design without decorations made by Paul Revere about 1790–1800.

53. Fluted and engraved teapot with stand by Paul Revere, the patriot, Boston, about 1780. Delicate Adam influence.

54. Sugar basket by Adam Lynn, Alexandria, Va., late eighteenth century. Adam influence in silver design.

By 1800 the classic style had reached its height in America. Architecture, furniture, and silver were made in the simple and delicate designs that had originated with the Adam brothers in London. These designs seemed to fit the young country because they seemed to match it. The vogue continued through the first quarter of the century. Then came the end of the period of really good design in American silver. A new and disturbing element overtook the work of even the best craftsmen. There was a reason for this, just as there was a reason for the early designs of silver spoons, the small teapots, and the decorations in the classic styles. That was the Machine

*55. Service with tea- and coffeepot by John Mc-
Mullin and H. Erwin, Philadelphia, about
1790. Pierced-gallery.*

56. *Three-piece tea set by Daniel Van Voorhis, Philadelphia (1751–1824). Fine sets made there in late eighteenth century.*

57. *Large sugar urn by Christian Wiltberger, Philadelphia, late eighteenth century. Adam influence and pierced decoration.*

58. *Tea set made by Jacob G. Lansing working in Albany, New York, from 1765 to 1803.*

59. *Tea set by Standish Barry, Baltimore, Md. He worked from 1784 into 1800s. Suggests the Phila-delphia designs.*

62.

60. *A graceful sugar and creamer with definite Adam influence made by Freeman Woods, N. Y., 1791–1793.*

Age which began an upset that is still in process.

During the first quarter of the nineteenth century most of the distinguished craftsmen were aging or had retired or had died. Although new men were still trained in the apprentice system, a change in the mode of living was taking place and with it came a change in design and workmanship. By 1830 America was on the move. There were canals and railroads to take the people from the eastern seaboard to new lands that were being opened in the West. Many things like furniture and silver, which had been made entirely by hand, were being produced, in part at least, by some new and wonderful machine. If

61. Tea set with waste bowl and tongs by Isaac Hutton, Albany, N. Y., about 1800. Albany Institute of History and Art.

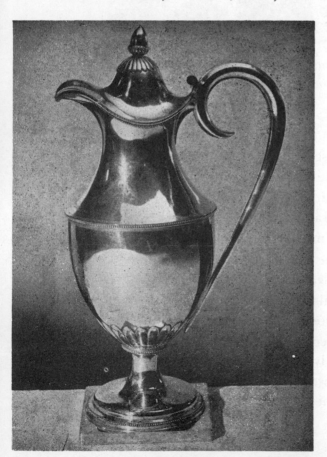

62. Covered jug made by Isaac Hutton, Albany, N. Y., about 1790. Albany Institute of History and Art.

63. *Finely engraved tea set made by Abraham Du Bois, Philadelphia, in 1787.*

you did not care for a plain house, simple furniture, and austere silver, but wanted ornament, it could be turned out cheaply and quickly by the machine. Poor workmanship could also be covered up by the machine. By 1840 in this country, in England, and even on the Continent work was being turned out by the machine that would not have been accepted twenty-five years before.

Although Victoria came to the throne of England in 1837, we cannot blame everything in poor taste upon the Queen. She probably was not amused at many things that happened in her long reign, when the machine ruled the world and design reached a low ebb.

Let us say plainly, however, that there is noth-

64. *Chalices, 1790, by Miles Beach, Litchfield and Hartford, Conn. Gift of Dr. Joseph Wells to First Church of Berlin, Conn.*

ing essentially wrong with machines. They are needed and always will be, but they never have and never will take the place of the skilled hand. Proof of this is readily seen in the work of the many small handicraft shops that have been started all over the country in the last forty

65. *Tea set by Isaac Hutton, Albany, N. Y., about 1800. Helmet pitcher. Fine engraving. Albany Institute of History and Art.*

66. Oval rib-fluted teapot with urn finial, by Isaac Hutton, about 1810. Albany Institute of History and Art.

years. The finest furniture, silver, and jewelry are made by hand and some handwork must usually be done even on machine products to give a good finish.

But as the nation moved and grew, and machine work supplanted handwork, and railroads and waterways opened new ways to wealth, more people demanded things that looked elegant, even if the workmanship was not of the finest. Furniture got heavier and richer, silver for the great sideboards got larger and was more ornamented. When this big silver was too expensive, the machine offered plated ware that looked just as fine to the untrained eye. Perhaps the best way to explain the nineteenth century is to say it surrendered to mass production.

67. *Tea set of good design made by Joel Sayre, New York, and dated 1808.*

68. *Tray by George Riggs, Georgetown, D. C., 1804.*

68.

69. Tea and coffee set by Abraham Carlisle of Philadelphia, 1790s. Tray is Sheffield plate and somewhat later.

PLATED AND STERLING SILVER

In the eighteenth century in England a process was developed at Sheffield for plating silver by fusing copper and pure silver at great heat. Copper-plated silver has always been known as Sheffield plate, although it was later made in quantity in Birmingham. The Sheffield process was not like that developed in England in the nineteenth century and known today as electroplating. By this process a coating of silver was put on a finished article of base metal, sometimes copper but later various kinds of white metal.

69.

70. *Tea set by Robert Shepherd of Albany, N. Y., about 1810. Sheffield plated tray of the same period.*

The silver applied by electrolysis varied in weight with the factory. Some early plated silver still has the original surface; some pieces have been replated many times.

Genuine Sheffield plate when honestly made was of high quality. The story of the method and the objects it was applied to is told in Frederick Bradbury's *History of Sheffield Plate*. This is a large book full of detail and photographs, and though long out of print, may be found in many of the larger libraries.

Sheffield plate by the fusion process was not made in America, but factories here did turn out quantities of electroplated silver. In fact, it was so popular that one English firm with several variations of its name, but all including Dixon,

70.

sold quantities of electroplated silver, issued catalogues, and even had a New York showroom.

Today there is a great deal of American plated silver which has been treasured for years. Many families had plated silver as well as fine sterling. Some of it was inherited; some prized for sentimental reasons. If you have this plated ware, and it is as dear to you as fine early silver, then you are among the happy people of this world. Personal taste is just another of the freedoms.

A book has been written on American plated silver which includes a list of makers from the earliest days of the craft to well into the twentieth century. *Early American Plated Silver* by Larry Freeman and Jane Beaumont (published by Century House, Watkins Glen, New York) pictures hundreds of articles from catalogues, including tilting water pitchers, toothpick holders, napkin rings, and other elegancies of the Victorian era. Many small factories that made such wares in the mid-nineteenth century are now part of the International Silver Company, Meriden, Connecticut, which merged them in 1898.

On plated silver the terms "triple" and "quadruple" indicate the number of coatings received by the base metal in the electroplating process. Naturally the more metal used in the plating the longer the piece should last. Polishing and wear have taken their toll of much of this plated ware and whether pieces are worth replating depends on their usefulness and your pleasure in them. If you like them well enough to spend

71. Tea set by J. B. Jones & Co., Boston, about 1815. Design has little meaning, is neither good nor bad.

72. Tea set by William Thomson, New York City, about 1830. There is little fine design after this time.

72.

73. *Ornate tea service by R. & W. Wilson, Philadelphia, about 1835. Typical of design after 1830.*

74. *Teapot by William Gale & Son, New York City, in business from about 1825 to 1850.*

73.

75. *Presentation pieces, ornate pitcher and goblets, by William Adams, N. Y., 1852.*

money on them, then by all means have the work done, but remember a piece is worth at market value only the metal that is in it, the base metal under the plating being worth very little.

The word "Sterling" on American silver does not mean that the piece is old. The term was not in general use until the 1860s, when the standard of 925 parts fine silver and 75 parts of alloy was adopted. Pure silver would be too soft to work. The alloy is necessary to give strength to the metal. Before the mark "Sterling" was required the amount of pure silver varied from 900 to 925 parts fine. The early craftsmen made silver from coins which were not pure, and although they

74.

melted them down to assure quality silver, the metal was not always 925 parts silver. Design however compensated for lack of purity in the metal. Today when you buy reproduction silver and pay for sterling quality, be sure the mark is plainly stamped on every piece. Early silver usually has the mark of the silversmith who made it and his name was evidence of high standard.

III. SILVER TODAY—ANTIQUES AND REPRODUCTIONS

Interest in old silver seems to be almost universal. In the years that I have conducted a question-and-answer column on the antique pages of *The Sun* (now *New York World-Telegram and The Sun*), questions on American silver have come in from every state in the union, also from Canada, Hawaii, South America, and even from China. These queries have often been accompanied by "rubbings" of marks showing the name or initials of the maker.

If when seeking information by letter, you wish to send an exact description of a mark, make a drawing or rubbing in this way: Place a piece of tracing paper over the mark and rub over it with a medium-soft pencil. It will come through beautifully, giving the duplication necessary to show the size of the mark, the size and type of the letters, and any little distinguishing dots or marks peculiar to the silversmith. Often there are several makers who used the same initials, but each had his characteristics which show up in a clear mark.

If the mark is worn but can be clearly seen

under a strong magnifying glass, make a rubbing, but also print the name or initials beside the mark so the person who is trying to identify it can see the *shape of the enclosure* of the mark. This is most important for identification. You will understand all this better when you examine a book of silver marks and see how many of them appear alike. Careful examination, however, will reveal the *minor* differences between the mark on a rare early piece of silver and that on a more common piece, made perhaps a hundred or more years later.

Books with lists of makers are most helpful. A few years ago, many marks were unlisted, but today few are missing and we are fortunate in having books that give thousands of marks of men unknown even ten years ago.

Much reading should precede buying. A new and very complete book, published in 1948, is *American Silversmiths and Their Marks, III* by Stephen G. C. Ensko. That III after the title indicates that Mr. Ensko has published two other books on American marks, now unfortunately out of print. His father, Robert Ensko, also published a book of American silver marks in 1915, and many a collector today is indebted to him for his early knowledge of fine silver. With Mr. Ensko's book of marks and several other good books on American silver, plus frequent visits to museums, you can soon have a reliable background for the study of silver. And a very fascinating study it is.

The Hundred Masterpieces of American Silver in Public Collections by John Marshall Phillips of the Yale University Gallery of Fine Arts at New Haven, Connecticut, is another valuable book of reference. Reprinted from the magazine *Antiques,* it contains one hundred photographs of the rarest pieces to be seen in museums with a complete description of each piece, the maker, and museum containing it. A foreword describes the regional characteristics of eighteenth-century American silver.

Dr. Phillips has also written *American Silver,* printed in England and published in New York in 1949 by the Chanticleer Press. Several rare pieces are shown in color. This book will appeal especially to those collectors and students who already know something about the subject.

Then there are some excellent regional studies. Dr. George Barton Cutten has written about the silversmiths in and around Utica, New York, which he called, *The Silversmiths of Utica,* and has also compiled a list of makers, *The Silversmiths of the State of New York Outside New York City.* He has done a list of North Carolina silversmiths and is preparing one of those of Virginia.

Mr. E. Milby Burton, director of the Charleston Museum, has written a book on the South Carolina silversmiths from 1690 to 1860. Another regional book is *Silversmiths of Delaware, 1700–1850* by Miss Jessie Harrington and a monumental work is *Maryland Silversmiths* by J. Hall

Pleasants and Howard Sill. New Jersey is represented by Carl M. Williams' *Silversmiths of New Jersey, 1700–1825*. Other books will doubtless appear from various sections of the country and all will be welcome. With Stephen G. C. Ensko to keep us informed through revised books of marks, published every few years in limited editions, the study of silver becomes simpler now than it was a few years ago.

Toward the end of the eighteenth century many silversmiths were working in the cities and towns of the nation. By this time there were also skilled craftsmen in the South. In fact each section of the country produced its characteristic pieces, but that is a study in itself and we are grateful to the students of regional silver. Charleston, Baltimore, Wilmington, and even Alexandria, Virginia, had excellent craftsmen. These were coastal towns and such places had more trade and more desire for luxuries. Virginia, North Carolina, and other southern states did not seem to have men making silver in any quantity until the nineteenth century.

General books on silver are numerous and a few of the most popular are *Early American Silver* by C. Louise Avery, *Historic Silver of the Colonies and Its Makers* by F. H. Bigelow, and *The Practical Book of American Silver* by Edward Wenham.

For books with marks of American silversmiths the following are suggested: *Marks of Early American Silversmiths* by E. M. Currier, *A List*

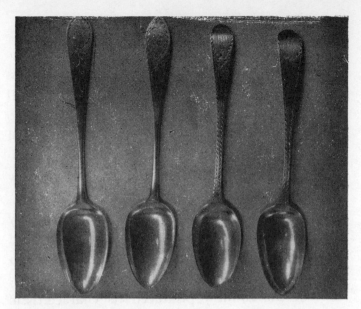

76. Spoons of the latter part of the nineteenth century, with the popular bright-cut and feather-edge engraving.

of *Early American Silversmiths and Their Marks* by Hollis French, *Early American Silver Marks* by James J. Graham, Jr., and *The Handbook of American Silver and Pewter Marks* by C. Jordan Thorn with thirty-five hundred marks. Some of these books are out of print, but may be found in libraries.

Many private collectors are generous with their collections and their knowledge, for no one can own and handle silver without learning much about it. Mr. and Mrs. Stanley B. Ineson of Man-

77. Ladle and sugar tongs with collectible Sheaf-of-Wheat and Basket-of Flowers designs, popular after 1810.

chester, Vermont, have a comprehensive and superior collection of spoons. Like Dr. Cutten of Chapel Hill, North Carolina, they have stressed quality as well as quantity and they have every type from the earliest spoons to those engraved with the popular Sheaf-of-Wheat and Basket-of-Flowers designs on the handles. These were first

81.

78. Table pieces collectible in Sheaf-of-Wheat and Basket-of-Flowers patterns.

made about 1810. Both collections have been shown in museums and it is hoped that in time books will be written about them.

Henry·F. du Pont, Esq. of Winterthur, Delaware, has one of the most important private collections of American silver. Eventually this will be open to the public. This silver is part of one of the finest collections of Americana owned by one person. It is arranged in a home with every detail correct as to period so it will be invaluable for the study of the nation's social history.

The late Francis P. Garvan, Esq. gave his superb collection of Americana, including many of the rarest examples of early American silver, to Yale, where it is known as the Mabel Brady Garvan Collection and may be seen at the Yale University Art Gallery.

82.

79. Fiddleback-with-Shell, designed by Fletcher and Gardiner, Philadelphia, about 1825. A collectible pattern.

OLD SILVER FOR MODERN COLLECTORS

Every year more and more pieces are being lent or given to museums and occasionally a fine private collection is sold at auction. There is still a considerable amount of good silver that may eventually come on the market and from this, new collections will be started. It has been said that each collection is broken up once every generation. If this is true, there is hope for those who wish to own at least a few pieces of fine silver.

Several years ago such an opportunity came in Cincinnati, Ohio, when at the death of W. T. H. Howe, Esq., his fine collection, including some

83.

excellent examples by Paul Revere, was sold at auction and many choice pieces became available to private collectors. This one event shows that if you learn about silver and watch the sales in reliable auction galleries, it is possible even today to acquire some really good American pieces.

Fortunately for collectors, everyone does not treasure heirlooms, and there are always those whose enthusiasms wane and who want something new. When a collection of silver is cleared out to make way for a different hobby, the new collector has a chance. Large museums also sometimes sell at auction pieces of which they have duplicates. Although the museum involved is seldom named, the catalogue usually states the original source from which the museum obtained the pieces. Whatever his source of supply, it is important for a collector, new or experienced, to learn as much as possible about the subject of silver in general, and then about the specific piece he contemplates adding to his collection.

FAMILY PIECES

Having read about silver, seen it in museums and perhaps in a few private collections, the average person invariably asks, "How can I hope to collect any antique silver today?" Certainly it can be done if you have time, patience, some money to spend, and do not expect to get the rarest and earliest pieces, most of which are in museums or private collections: However, there

84.

80. Late spoon by Storrs and Cook, Northampton, Mass., 1827 to 1833. Owner's initials on handle.

are still early, rare, and practically unknown pieces in families that have had them for generations, and someday they will pass on to another than the present owner, and it may be you. So there is hope. Part of the joy of collecting is in finding the unexpected. Perhaps in some relative's house there are early christening spoons being used for jelly, or old tablespoons in a kitchen drawer.

Many collectors start with interest in an heirloom which for years they took for granted, but which appears in a new light when compared with a piece in a museum or a shop. It may be a family teapot, a spoon, or a porringer which suggests the beginning of a set of spoons or a tea set or another porringer, to make a pair.

Families often buy silver for gifts, adding to a collection on special occasions. Sometimes parents buy silver for children while they are little and add to it when they marry. One family during the last ten years tried to get together two fine American tea sets for two small daughters.

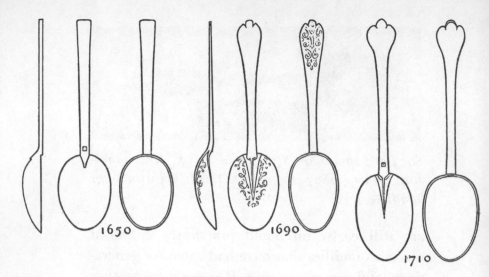

81a. Spoon designs from 1650 to 1710, details indicate approximate age.

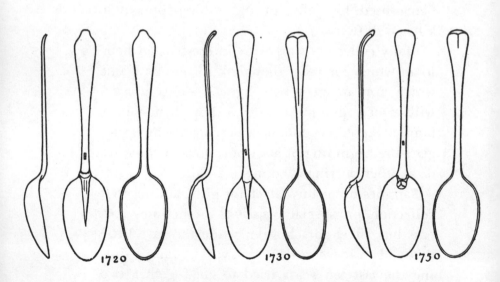

81b. Spoon designs from 1720 to 1750.

86.

Now when one is married, her set is all complete. Perhaps today it might not be easy to get a complete set just when it is needed. It is best to buy a piece when it comes on the market; too many rarities have been lost through waiting. First learn about what you have in the family and develop a working knowledge of silver before you buy. You will keep learning, but you should know something about designs and makers before you buy even a single piece.

Mr. and Mrs. Stanley B. Ineson, of Manchester, Vermont, who have more than two thousand antique silver spoons, started with some old spoons they inherited. They grew interested in the various types and before they knew it they were adding to the family silver. Fortunately they learned all they could about spoons and silversmiths and have bought wisely, but the collection started in a modest way.

It is still possible to get together a good silver tea set, one piece at a time. Sometimes with patience and the help of a reliable dealer you can get pieces all by one maker, but remember complete tea sets, as we know them today, were not common until late in the eighteenth century. Still it is possible to get pieces of the same general style that go well together though they were made by different craftsmen. Naturally it is better to have pieces by one maker, but even original sets were often by different makers, the pieces being added at various times. The important thing is to have them of the same general design and workmanship.

You can still get a good teapot, small bowls for waste, creamers, sugar bowls with and without covers, or even those little open sugar baskets, popular in the late eighteenth and early nineteenth centuries. Many families have old silver spoons and these are suitable, if in period, to use with the tea settings. Trays for American tea sets have always been a problem. Few were made here and many fine American sets have been found with a tray of English silver or a good early Sheffield plate. If you have a family tea set of early workmanship and good quality, let a reliable dealer in antique silver advise you about the type of tray to use.

Good American spoons from 1775 to 1825 are still to be had and they make a fine collection both for use and enjoyment. There is always the possibility of finding some of those lovely little eighteenth-century teaspoons, many with bright-cut engraving or a feather edge for decoration. Some of the larger spoons, dessert and table size, are also lovely to own. There are ladles of all sizes by good makers, sugar tongs with engraved designs, bowls of all sizes, and pitchers, large and small. There are all types of mugs, wonderful baby gifts which can be passed along from one generation to another. There are even knives and forks of the early nineteenth century, some of them with the Sheaf-of-Wheat and Basket-of-Flowers designs found on spoons of the same period. Many collectors try to find knives, forks, and spoons with these designs by one maker. It has been done.

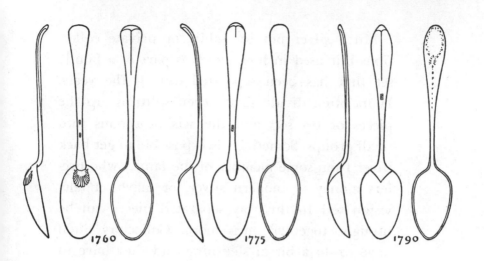

81c. Spoon designs from 1760 to 1790.

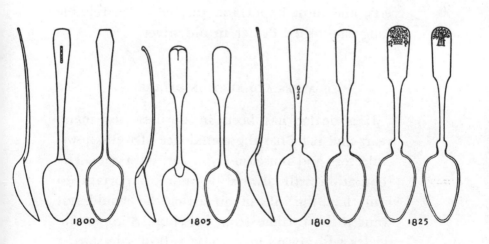

81d. Spoon designs from 1800 to 1825.

89.

Much silver not in public or private collections but used in households is part of a family set that has been separated during the years. Heirs often divide silver, even splitting up the pieces of tea sets and the sets of spoons into small groups. Sometimes it is possible to get back silver from some member of the family who prefers money or modern silver, or maybe a television set! In this way separated pieces can be brought together once more. Collectors often have to do a bit of sleuthing and they have to have plenty of patience and tact. In fact the true collector has to learn a lot of things, including the reasons why our ancestors did as they did, and there is no short road to knowledge of old silver any more than to any other subject. It takes time, interest, and the assistance of good friends in museums, of persons with like interests, and most important, the help of a reliable long-established dealer in old silver.

DEALERS AND AUCTION GALLERIES

If a dealer has been in business for many years and if he has the confidence of well-known collectors and museums, you can trust him. His reputation will always be more important to him than the sale of an article he would not want to have come from his shop. A reputable dealer will always give you a bill of sale stating plainly what you have bought and by whom it was made, if it is marked. If he is not willing to do this, do not buy from him. No honest dealer would put his name on a bill for silver that was not what he claimed it was. This bill is not only your proof of what you buy, it is also his good will and a record of your silver for tax and inheritance purposes.

If you get in the habit of going to a reliable dealer, let him know that you are serious about buying, but also tell him that you want to learn. To show good faith, do not take up too much of his time without making a purchase once in a while. It will be his pleasure to give you the best he can for the amount you wish to spend. He would like you for a customer and he would also like to see you get what you want. You will find that the average dealer is a pretty nice person. He likes his work or he would not have a shop. He gets fine things because he knows them and you are sharing his knowledge and his good taste. Do not buy from any shop which uses high-pressure salesmanship. Old silver like other things of value should never be bought quickly or without due consideration.

You can also buy from auction galleries of established reputation. Catalogues clearly state what a piece is and if it is not what it is claimed to be, the galleries are obliged to refund your money. Naturally they make few mistakes. It is wise to examine goods offered for sale.

Your dealer will show you how to use a book of marks and will help you identify a piece of silver even if you have not bought it from him. If you want to buy at auction and are not sure of how to do it, you can have your dealer buy for you at a small percentage and even so you will probably save money. A dealer is used to buying at auction; you still have to learn, and it takes knowing. You could even sit in the gallery while he buys a piece or two. This will be an education for you. In a short while you will learn not to be overeager and so pay out of proportion to worth. The uninitiated should leave auction-buying to the experienced. It is a highly specialized business. Many collectors of the choicest silver leave buying at auction to a favorite dealer.

However you buy, avoid accumulating silver you cannot use or enjoy. This is not true collecting. Acquire one good piece rather than several not of the best design or workmanship. Have a good reason for collecting; strive not for quantity but quality. Buy the best you can afford and study as you buy. Learn about silver from every source available. Go often to museums where collections are on view. Watch for the acquisitions and always remember—silver is a good investment, one of the few material things that will increase in value with the years.

REBIRTH OF DESIGN

Design started on its downward path in the nineteenth century soon after the machine became important and design grew steadily worse throughout the century. It passed through periods facetiously known as the General Grant, the Golden Oak, and the Mission, and on to something that has been called Early Halloween. Not until the twentieth century did manufacturers begin to see that the designs of a hundred or more years ago were good and could stand repeating.

It is said that some of our famous collectors of antique silver first saw its beauty at the Philadelphia Centennial in 1876. There in a series of huge buildings was exhibited everything the machine could do. Catalogues from that exhibition are amazing with pictures of objects ugly beyond understanding. Ostentation and size were the criteria of the day. But among all the machine-made objects were displayed some furniture, glass, and silver of the century before, the time of the American Revolution. Persons of discernment who were not engulfed by the taste of 1876 stopped to admire those exhibits, which were not called antiques at that time.

The late Henry W. Erving of Hartford, Connecticut, as a young man went to the Centennial and he said afterward that he made up his mind then to find out more about eighteenth-century things and to get some. Many will recall that when Mr. Erving died a few years ago he had one of the outstanding collections of furniture, glass, and silver in the country. Many of his pieces have been shown in books on antiques.

Although his collections were not so large as some today, he had only the choicest items.

Another man who at that time began to wonder about the craftsmanship of a hundred years or more before 1876 was Dr. Irving W. Lyon, also of Hartford, who studied and collected antiques and also wrote a book which is now famous, *The Colonial Furniture of New England*. Dr. Lyon began collecting in 1877 and he, too, became interested in early silver. In turn his son, Charles Woolsey Lyon, collected and was one of the pioneer antiques dealers in New York City. From him many early collectors bought choice things that are now in museums or noted collections.

Men such as these started the trend back to the appreciation of the crafts of the eighteenth century. Mr. Erving said that when he started housekeeping in the 1870s, he could not afford the furnishings in vogue so he had to buy "secondhand" things. At that time many a family had discarded the beautiful mahogany and delicate silver of earlier days for the heavy styles of the 1870s and 1880s. Thus the finer things found their way into secondhand concerns. There were no antiques shops then, but small stores where used furniture, mirrors, and even silver were sold cheaply because few wanted to be out of fashion. It was the very few like Mr. Erving and Dr. Lyon, with appreciation for the fine workmanship of a hundred years before, who paved the way for a renaissance of good design. They began to study the workmanship of the past and to interest others in it. In a few years these men were lending their possessions to museums and historical societies and more people showed an interest in collecting. It took years, however, before much was known about the origin of fine silver, since there were then no books of reference.

While bad design persisted through the 1890s and into the 1900s, interest gradually increased in old designs, and in the 1900s there seems to have been a rebirth of appreciation. It did not reach far at first, but the late R. T. H. Halsey, and a few others, began to collect fine furniture and silver. Mr. Halsey was even instrumental in arranging an exhibition of old silver in Boston in 1906. This was the first time the public realized that beautiful handmade silver had been produced centuries before. Those who had inherited it had been taking it for granted and it had previously had little value for them except as it was useful. After this first important exhibition of American silver knowledge and interest in collecting grew.

Perhaps the greatest impetus to appreciation of our artistic heritage was the opening of the American Wing in the Metropolitan Museum of Art in New York in 1922. This series of fine rooms, furnished in detail with the furniture, mirrors, glass, paintings, and silver of the past aroused the public in general and designers in particular to the beauty of it all. It was Mr. Halsey who gave further stimulus with *Homes of Our Ancestors,* the book he wrote with Elizabeth Tower, who later became his wife. The Wing and this book no doubt were contributing factors in the rebirth of good design.

Today most silver is made by machine but much of it copies the good designs of the past. There are even a few craftsmen who fashion it by hand, but labor costs are so high that then the final price is too great for general distribution. But what about reproductions of old silver? Certainly there is good reproduction silver on the market. The best is faithfully copied from known old pieces by important early makers. Some reproductions bear the name of the modern maker and the name of the silversmith from whose work the design is copied. There are some excellent copies of bowls, pitchers, and teapots from those made by Paul Revere, and there are also exact copies of the work of other early silversmiths including pieces by John Coney. Next to having really old pieces made by early craftsmen, an honest copy in high quality silver is desirable.

Unfortunately many large factories which can well afford to educate taste are turning out patterns, usually for table settings, which are over-ornamented or just pretty. Extensive catalogues are issued picturing the designs, but among them are some simple pleasing patterns which have

96.

stood the test of time. Some of the designs used in the late eighteenth and early nineteenth centuries have kept their popularity through the years and may be found in the better shops today. The simple thread pattern, the shell design, and the unornamented designs of the late eighteenth century can be bought today. Few fancy patterns stay long in vogue and in a few years it is often impossible to add pieces to a set; simple patterns, often just good copies of old silver, seem to last through the years.

Today some dealers in antique silver have added fine copies of old pieces to their stock. These copies are marked as such and are for those who prefer old silver but do not want to pay the price for it. These copies make excellent gifts for weddings and christenings, and their quality is so high that they become heirlooms of the future.

When you buy reproductions of antique silver, be sure you are getting exact copies and not adaptations, which usually have little to recommend them, being neither very good nor very bad. Study pieces of worth-while antique silver before you buy a reproduction. Then you will know what a sincere copy should look like.

IV. MARKS AND MAKERS

The marks of early American silversmiths are interesting but it takes study to know them. Many silversmiths used marks that look alike to the untrained eye, but each had some little characteristic that differentiates it—the shape of the letters or of one letter, a dot, or the type of enclosure around name or initials. With a small but powerful magnifying glass you can bring each mark into sharp focus and compare it in detail with those shown in books of silver marks.

The period of time in which each craftsman worked and the type of pieces he made constitute an important part of your knowledge of old silver. If you know when a man worked and if the mark on a certain piece agrees with his dates, you can be fairly sure of attributing the silver in question. When in doubt consult someone in your nearest museum or see your friend and mentor, the reliable dealer in antique silver.

Always remember that a fine piece of antique silver is a good investment, that its value will increase with the years. Many persons have bought old silver for investment and if it was from a re-

MARKS OF EARLY AMERICAN SILVERSMITHS

Mark	Name	Location	Date
R.&A.CAMPBELL	R. & A. Campbell B.M.	Baltimore, Md.	1835
RA.LYTLE 1015	R. A. Lytle B.M.	Baltimore, Md.	1825
RB	Roswell Bartholomew	Hartford, Conn.	1805
RB RB	Robert Brookhouse	Salem, Mass.	1800
R.BEAUVAIS	Rene Beauvais	St. Louis, Mo.	1838
RBROWN ★ 10·15	Robert Brown	Baltimore, Md.	1813
R.BROWN & SON	R. J. Brown & Son	Boston	1833
RC	Robert Campbell B.M.	Baltimore, Md.	1819

	Name	City	Date
R·C	Richard Conyers	Boston	1688
RD	Robert Douglas	New London, Conn.	1766
RD	Richard Van Dyke	New York	1750
RE RE	Robert Evans	Boston	1798
REEVES	Enos Reeves	Charleston, S. C.	1784
RE·SMITH	Richard E. Smith	Louisville, Ky.	1827
REVANS	Robert Evans	Boston	1798
REVERE ·REVERE	Paul Revere	Boston	1757
RF	Rufus Farnam	Boston	1796

Mark	Maker	Location	Date
R.F RF	Robert Fairchild	Durham, Conn.	1740
R.FAIRCHILD	Robert Fairchild	Durham, Conn.	1740
R.FARNAM	Rufus Farnam	Boston	1796
R.G	Robert Gray	Portsmouth, N. H.	1830
E.E.BAILEY	E. E. Bailey	Portland, Me.	1825
EE&SC BAILEY	E. E. & S. C. Bailey	Portland, Me.	1830
E.G	Eliakim Garretson	Wilmington, Del.	1785
E.GARRETSON	Eliakim Garretson	Wilmington, Del.	1785
E.Gifford	E. Gifford	Fall River, Mass.	1825

Mark	Maker	Location	Date
E·GUNN	Enos Gunn	Waterbury, Conn.	1792
EH	Eliphaz Hart	Norwich, Conn.	1810
E·H EH	Eliakim Hitchcock	New Haven, Conn.	1757
E·HART	Eliphaz Hart	Norwich, Conn.	1810
E&H	Euff & Howell	New York	1805
E·HOLSEY	E. Holsey	Philadelphia	1820
E·HUGHES	Edmund Hughes	Middletown, Conn.	1804
E.J.AUSTIN	Ebenezer J. Austin	Charlestown, Mass.	1760
E JEFFERIS	Enmor Jefferis	Wilmington, Del.	1827

Mark	Silversmith	Location	Date
E JEFFERSON	Ephraim Jefferson	Smyrna, Del.	1815
E JONES	Elisha Jones	New York	1827
E K LAKEMAN	E. K. Lakeman	Salem, Mass.	1830
EL	Edward Lang	Salem, Mass.	1763
E L BAILEY & CO	E. L. Bailey & Co.	Claremont, N. H.	1835
E LESCURE	Edward P. Lescure	Philadelphia	1822

Marks of Early American Silversmiths from AMERICAN SILVERSMITHS AND THEIR MARKS, III, *1948, by permission of the author, Stephen G. C. Ensko.*

liable dealer or has come with an authenticated family history, its value increased in the course of time far beyond the original cost. Actually owning fine silver is like having money in the bank; the very metal from which it is made has value.

Perhaps the best example of what one man thought of the value of a silver collection was shown by the late Francis P. Garvan who gave the Garvan Collection to Yale University. When the Victoria and Albert Museum in London asked him to lend his collection, he replied that he would be glad to if the museum would send a battleship for it and would return it the same way. This famous collector knew the intrinsic as well as the esthetic value of his silver.

THE BEAUTY OF OLD SILVER

Why is old silver beautiful? First of all, it was handmade and has individuality. Second, it has a patina that old metals and woods acquire with years of hand-rubbing and exposure to light and air. Third, all the decoration that was applied to old silver was done by some expert engraver who followed the contours of the piece, adding to its beauty. Silver, like all precious metals, appeals to everyone who sees it because it suggests the luxury of good living.

Modern silver is rolled out by mechanical pressure that takes much of the life out of it. Old silver was handmade from the time the coins were melted until the piece was ready for use. It was hammered, shaped, heated, and worked with great patience until it acquired some flavor of the maker's personality.

Note how simple the finest pieces of old silver are. Note the hammer marks that were carefully polished but not erased. Examine carefully the delicate flutes on coffee- and teapots, the tiny feet of cream pitchers, the handles of exquisite workmanship on tankards and mugs. There is much to study in the diversified engraving on all types of silver, especially in the work of the craftsmen of the late eighteenth century. Examine the many kinds of finials on tea- and coffeepots, sugar bowls, or any covered piece. Most of them are beautifully wrought, as are all the other fine details.

Indeed, intrinsic value is rarely the stimulus for collecting old silver. The beauty of the pieces, the sentiment each holds, the very feel of the smooth surfaces—these are the reasons for collecting.

V. MUSEUMS TO VISIT

Today's museum is no longer a stuffy institution but a place where exhibits are well arranged and well lighted and where trained staffs gladly help the public to understand the exhibits and to solve problems of personal interest. Director, curators, and personnel are highly trained. Many do research and write articles and books about various phases of their subjects. A fine working library is available to help with marks and makers.

Valuations of old silver, however, are not the province of a museum. In any case there are no fixed values for silver and museums do not buy and sell as dealers do. Silver acquired by museums comes through gifts or through purchase from reputable dealers and at auctions. Museums buy in the open market just as individuals do.

The museum is there for you. Learn to use it and to enjoy it. Learn to know the staff and show your appreciation for their interest. Even the larger institutions are more or less dependent on the public for loans and gifts. The largest public museum in this country is, of course, the Metropolitan Museum of Art in New York City. Here in the American Wing with its paneled rooms taken from famous houses you will see the silver of the time and place. Special exhibits of fine silver are also held here with many examples of the work of New York craftsmen.

The Museum of Fine Arts in Boston is rich in examples of the work of Boston and other New England silversmiths. There is also a special permanent exhibit of the work of Paul Revere, his tools, and his portrait by John Singleton Copley. Revere's descendants have been generous with his silver and the curators, Edwin J. Hipkiss and Mrs. Henry Yves Buhler, have managed to find the finest pieces possible for the Museum.

The Museum of the City of New York and the New-York Historical Society, both in New York City, have much fine American silver, particularly that made by New York craftsmen.

The Albany Institute of History and Art has a good collection particularly representative of Albany silversmiths. This museum has done considerable research on local craftsmen and is adding their work to its collection.

The Yale University Art Gallery, New Haven, under the direction of Dr. John Marshall Phillips, owns the outstanding Garvan Collection of rare American silver, including the unique gold spoons made by Simeon Soumaine (1685–1765).

The Philadelphia Museum of Art has American silver with quantities of the best work of the Philadelphia makers. During the late eighteenth century, just before and at the time when that city was the capital of the nation, its silversmiths turned out a great deal of beautiful work including many fine complete tea sets.

The Baltimore Museum of Art is noted for examples of the work of Baltimore and Annapolis silversmiths and also of men who worked on the Eastern Shore of Maryland.

The Worcester (Massachusetts) Art Museum and the Rhode Island School of Design in Providence have good collections of American silver and examples of the work of local makers.

While the majority of the early silversmiths worked in the East, silver, like everything else, moved west so there is much of it in museums far from the places where it was made. The Detroit Institute of Arts, the Cleveland Museum of Arts, the Minneapolis Institute of Arts, and Chicago Art Institute all have important collections.

Farther west, there are collections in the City Art Museum at St. Louis, Missouri, and in the William Rockhill Nelson Gallery of Art in Kansas City, Missouri.

Many smaller museums and historical and patriotic societies over the country have American silver of which they are proud. Often extremely rare pieces are found in these smaller collections.

Incidentally those who own fine silver should know that museums are grateful for loans of personal collections or even single pieces of quality. They especially welcome examples of local interest and pieces of historical significance and they offer a safe place in which to share your silver.

If you own family silver or have acquired a collection, you will eventually have to think about its disposal. If you have the history of your silver, be sure it is in writing so that there will be an authentic record for those who inherit it. This is important. It is your contribution to posterity. Your will should also definitely direct to whom your silver is to go. Keep in mind that if you give your treasures to a museum, you will be bringing knowledge and delight to many people.

VI. BOOKS TO READ

Books about old silver have been written in this country since the 1880s. True, more were written about English than American silver, but those early books which may be seen today in libraries were the pioneer texts.

Unfortunately few were interested in American silver thirty years ago, so many good books were published only in limited editions and some were privately printed. Such books soon went into private, public, or museum libraries and to collectors. When the layman wanted a book about silver he either had to go to a library for it or to a shop carrying out-of-print books, and often he had to pay many times the original cost for the book he desired. During the last few years some of these older books on silver have brought fabulous prices at auction sales.

Today publishers realize the wide interest in American silver. They are bringing out books on the subject at reasonable prices and in large enough editions so they will not soon be out of print. A few of the better older books have been reprinted and these sell at a reasonable price.

Stephen G. C. Ensko's *American Silversmiths*

and Their Marks, III, published in 1948, is the newest and most comprehensive book of American makers. (Mr. Ensko's other two books are long out of print.) This book includes not only all the known marks but has biographical items on the various makers, also maps of Boston, Philadelphia, and New York, showing the places where the early craftsmen in silver worked.

The Book of Old Silver by Seymour Wyler is a popular book at a moderate cost and still in print. It is not only about American silver but has marks of English and foreign silversmiths and information about them.

Early American Silver Marks by James Graham, Jr. was privately printed in 1936 and may be found in most libraries.

Most of the larger libraries have not only books on American silver but also on file many articles in magazines and newspapers. These are valuable because they include research material not yet published in book form. Helen Burr Smith, Mrs. John Russel Hastings, and Dr. Phillips have done invaluable research in the last few years from original records. There are also monographs on such silversmiths as Coney, Winslow, and Dummer, and much has been written on Paul Revere as a silversmith. Catalogues of silver exhibitions are also filed in libraries and these have valuable information and also photographs.

Let your librarian help to find books on early American silver. Go to the museums and to auction sales and use the books of reference to interpret what you see. You have a whole new world before you.

VII. TERMS TO KNOW

Bright-cut. A type of engraving on metal in which the design is lightly cut so as to produce à reflecting surface. This popular decoration was used by silversmiths in the late eighteenth century, especially on spoons.

Buckles. Shoe and knee buckles were popular in the eighteenth century, and are highly prized by collectors today. Many silversmiths made buckles and they are often found with the marks of prominent makers.

Can. A drinking vessel with a handle, and usually with a rounded bottom and molded base.

Caster. An article resembling a modern pepper and salt shaker, but usually larger. It was first used for sugar, later for salt. Casters were made in various shapes and sizes, often with a finial.

Caudle Cup. A two-handled bowl-like cup, sometimes with a cover. It was used for various beverages but mostly for caudle, a drink of wine or ale, heated, and mixed with bread, sugar, spices, and sometimes eggs.

Chasing. Decoration on the surface of silver made by tools without a cutting edge. In chasing, the metal is displaced by pressure. (Cf. *engraving* which removes part of the metal with a sharp tool.)

Coffin-End Spoon. A popular type named for its handle which resembled a wooden coffin of about 1800. Originally these spoons may have been given as gifts to pallbearers, but "funeral" spoons were earlier and more elaborate. The term "coffin-end" probably came from the shape of the handle rather than a connection with funerals.

Cut-Card Work. A decoration of silver cut from a separate piece of metal and applied as a design. Some cut-card work was simple and some intricately pierced and lacelike. Many fine tankards have cut-card decoration at the base.

Engraving. Decoration on the surface of silver

made by a sharp tool. This popular type of decoration was used for names, initials, monograms, and cyphers, as well as for floral and conventional motifs. Paul Revere was an expert engraver, but many silversmiths had to have their engraving done by others. (Cf. *chasing*, which is decoration by pressure and without cutting.)

Flatware. Spoons, knives, and forks. (Cf. *hollow ware.*)

Hollow Ware. Such silver articles as teapots, coffeepots, pitchers, porringers, and bowls. (Cf. *flatware*, spoons, knives, and forks.)

Mark. An insignia on silver by which makers are identified. Names, initials, or such devices as a heart were used.

Mug. A drinking vessel resembling a tankard but usually smaller. It may have a cover. Mugs, cups, and cans are all drinking vessels with handles and the terms are interchanged. Perhaps the most popular name today for any small drinking vessel with a handle is "mug."

Porringer. A dish used for various solid foods and also for liquids. This was one of the most useful articles ever made by the early silversmiths. Almost every Colonial household had a porringer of pewter if not of silver. Porringers were given to brides and babies as gifts and were cherished and passed down in families. They are often mentioned in old wills, showing how important they were. Most of the early silversmiths made porringers and, because they were popular over such a long period, it is still possible to buy interesting silver ones with good marks.

Posset. A beverage made from curdled milk mixed with hot wine or ale, spices, and small pieces of bread or oaten cakes. It was often drunk from a caudle cup.

Rattail Spoon. So-called for the narrow raised silver piece at the back of the bowl. The device may have been used to give strength. Many silversmiths employed the rattail motif decoratively in finely wrought designs.

Repoussé. Relief decoration usually on thin silver, the design being raised by hammering from the inside. Many of the earliest two-handled cups have repoussé decoration on the lower part.

Spoon. A utensil of great antiquity, possibly first made of shells, horn, or wood. The earliest American type is known today as the Puritan spoon although it was not so called when it was first made. It is rather crude with a large rounded bowl and a straight handle, thin and rather long. It is not beautiful as are later spoons but prized for rarity.

Sterling. A type of modern silver that is 925 parts fine. Pure silver is 1,000 parts fine and too soft for general use. The word "sterling" is believed to have originated with a German tribe called Easterling, famous for the purity of its silver in the Middle Ages. Sterling was the standard for English silver, but American smiths had no laws to compel them to make silver of this standard. However, most of them were honest and tried to make high-quality silver to compete with that of English contemporaries. About 1865 a law was passed requiring all silver to be stamped *Sterling,* if it was 925 parts fine; otherwise it could not bear the stamp. At that time there was so much plated silver being made that it was necessary to use the stamp to distinguish the two types.

Tankard. A drinking vessel with handle and lid and having a thumbpiece to facilitate the raising of the cover. Most tankards are large but some rare small ones have been found which are believed to have been made for women or children. Designs varied with locality and silversmith.

Thumbpiece. A decorative device to raise the lid of a tankard. It was simple or elaborate and often with an unusual motif—animal or bird, even the eagle. The study of the designs of thumbpieces is endless and fascinating.

Trifid-End Spoon. An early type of spoon with two notches or indentations at the tip of the handle. This was not popular over a long period because the notches wore down and caught in linen as they were sharp. This style was followed by the rounded handle.

ABOUT THE AUTHOR

Millicent Stow (Mrs. Charles Messer Stow) has for many years been associated with the field of antiques. She has known personally the principal figures in it, has had opportunity to examine at leisure both private and public collections, and has attended numerous forums, symposiums, and the important auctions. In addition to constant exposure to expert opinion, she has been made continuously aware of the amateur's interest and problems. Through her column in the New York *Sun* she has answered thousands of questions—particularly about silver. Through readers' descriptions and "rubbings" of marks, she has helped them to identify many family pieces, and so set many an amateur on the road to collecting.

Mrs. Stow continues to contribute to the Antiquarian Department of the New York *World-Telegram and Sun,* of which her husband is antiquarian editor. She also writes articles on antiques for various magazines and is the author of a delightfully informing booklet, *Early American Silver,* in the *Enjoy Your Museum* series.

INDEX